ESSENTIAL ELEMENTS

GUITAR ENSEMBLES

ROCK INSTRUMENTALS

CONTENTS

Arrangements by Mark Phillips

ISBN 978-1-4803-6044-0

HAL•LEONARD® CORPORATION

7777 W. BLUEMOUND RD. P.O. BOX 13819 MILWAUKEE, WI 53213

Visit Hal Leonard Online at
www.halleonard.com

BECK'S BOLERO

By Jimmy Page

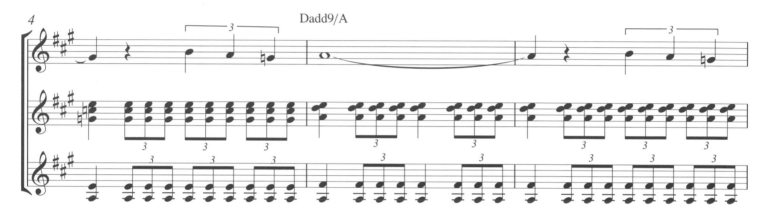

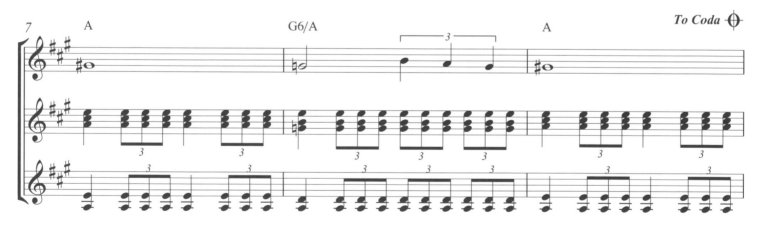

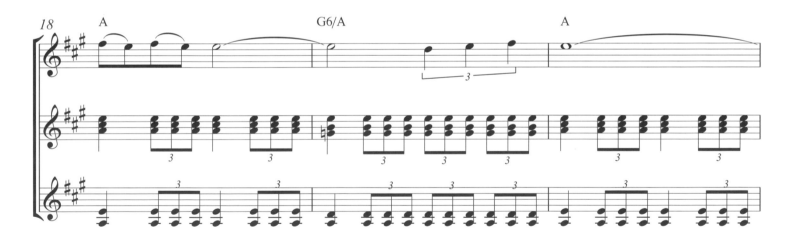

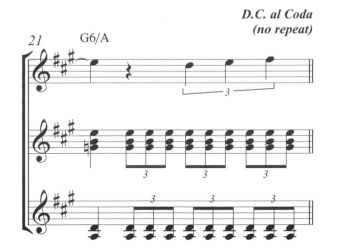

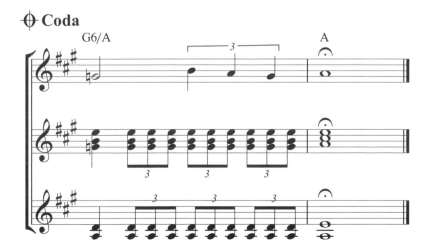

CISSY STRUT

By Arthur Neville, Leo Nocentelli, George Porter and Joseph Modeliste, Jr.

PIPELINE

By Bob Spickard and Brian Carman

*Slide down from
15th fret, 6th string,
while rapidly and
continuously picking.

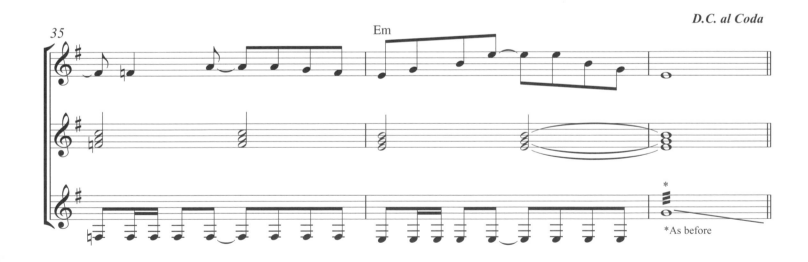

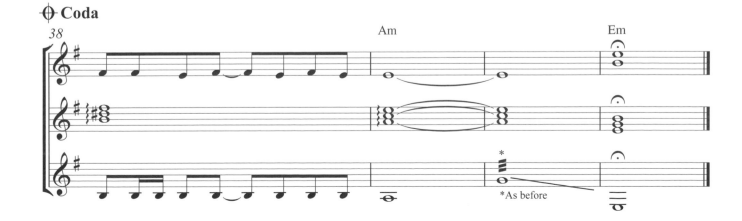

EUROPA
(Earth's Cry Heaven's Smile)
Words and Music by Carlos Santana and Tom Coster

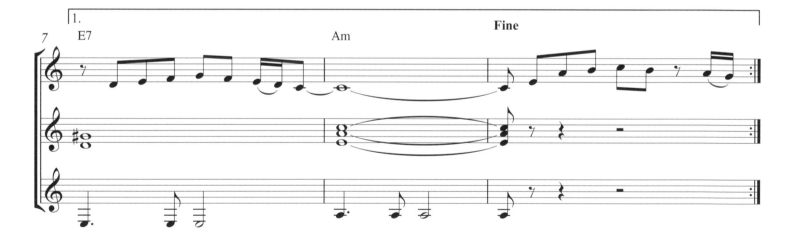

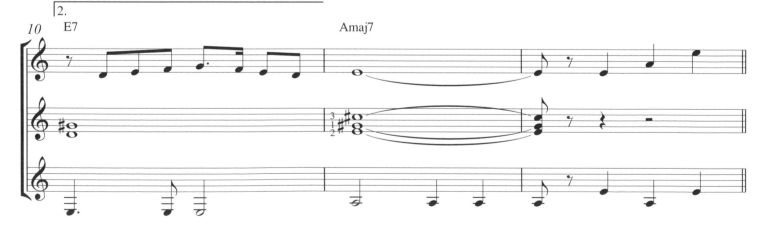

B

D.S. al Fine
(take 1st ending)

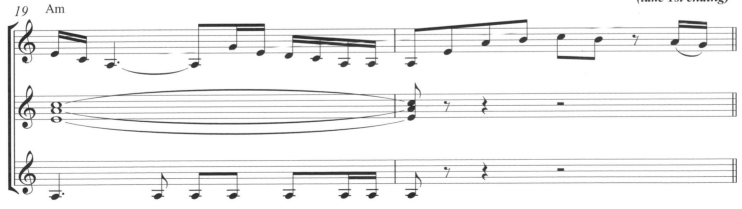

FRANKENSTEIN
By Edgar Winter

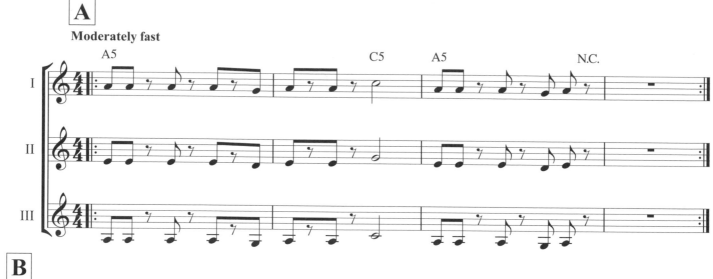

GREEN ONIONS

Written by Al Jackson, Jr., Lewis Steinberg, Booker T. Jones and Steve Cropper

JESSICA
Words and Music by Dickey Betts

MISIRLOU

Words by Fred Wise, Milton Leeds, Jose Pina and Sidney Russell
Music by Nicolas Roubanis

*Tremolo picking. Pick
continuous sixteenth notes.

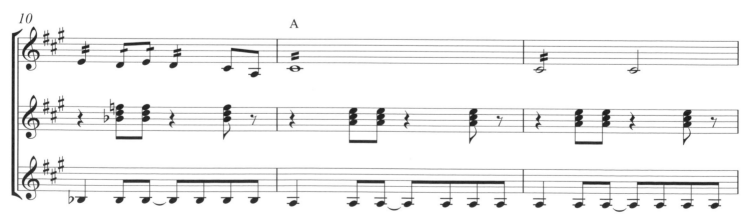

*Slide down from 14th fret, 3rd string,
while tremolo picking.

PERFIDIA

Words and Music by Alberto Dominguez

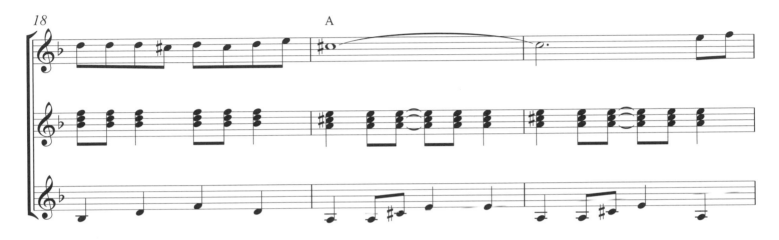

D.S. al Coda
(no repeat)

PICK UP THE PIECES

Words and Music by James Hamish Stuart, Alan Gorrie, Roger Ball, Robbie McIntosh, Owen McIntyre and Malcolm Duncan

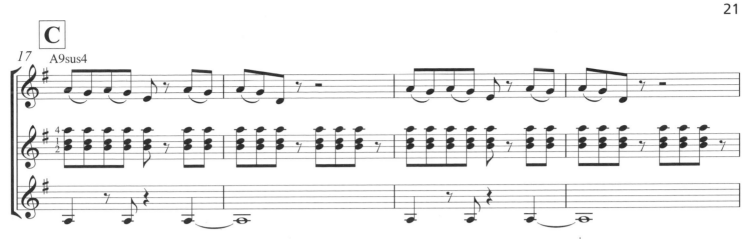

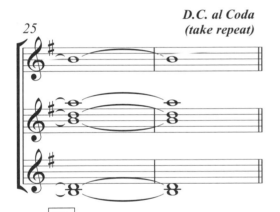

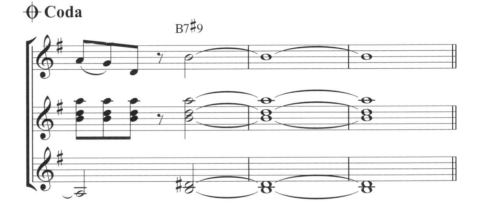

REBEL 'ROUSER
By Duane Eddy and Lee Hazlewood

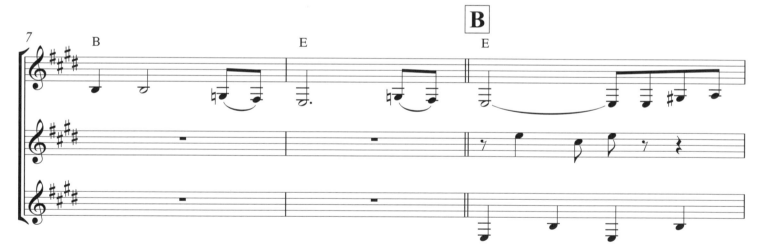

SLEEPWALK

By Santo Farina, John Farina and Ann Farina

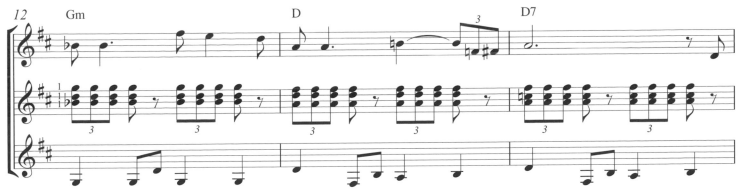

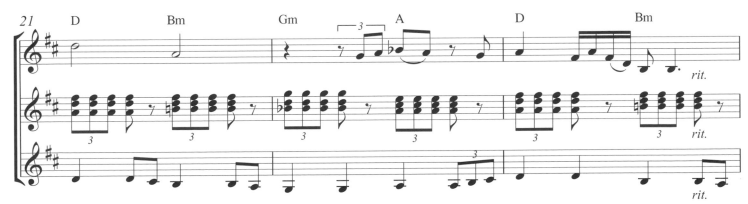

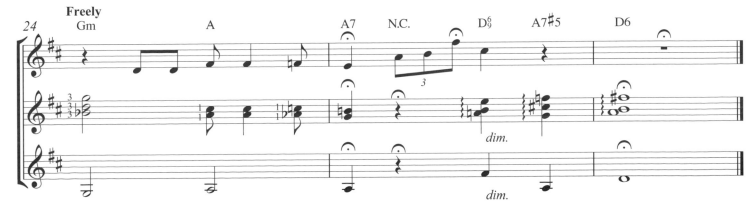

TEQUILA

By Chuck Rio

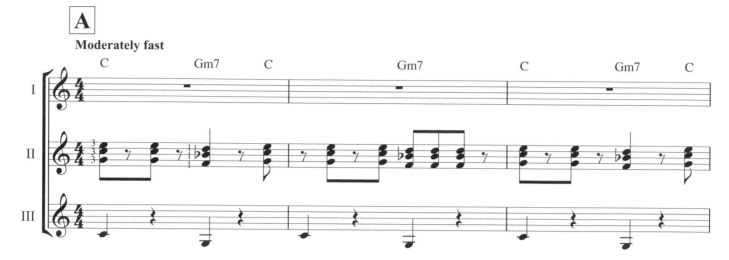

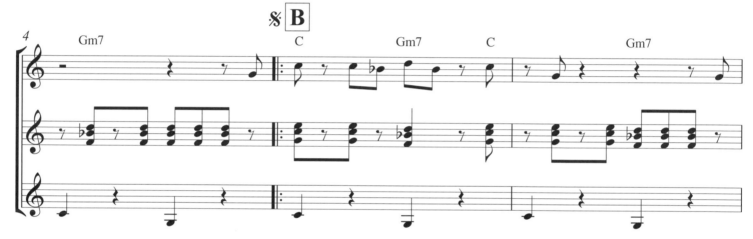

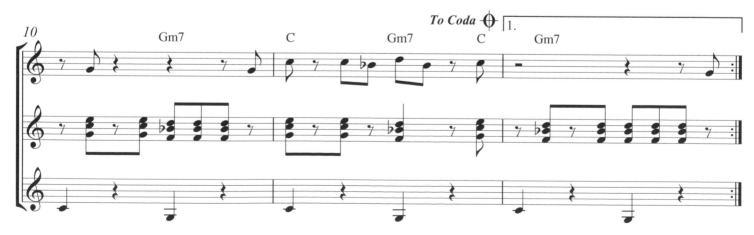

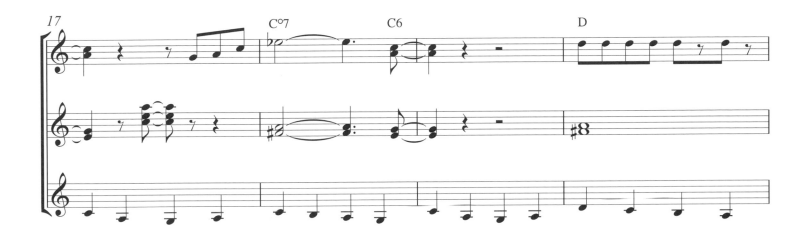

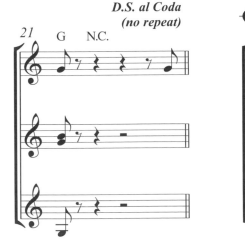

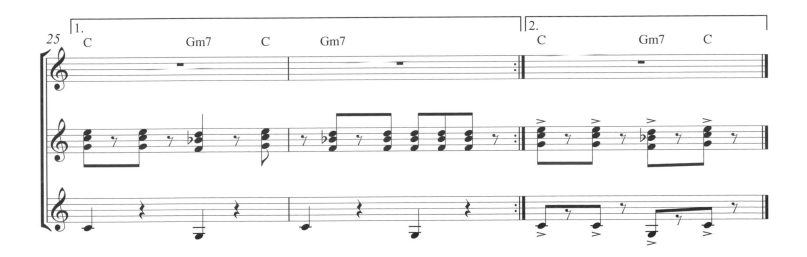

WALK DON'T RUN

By Johnny Smith

WIPE OUT

By The Surfaris

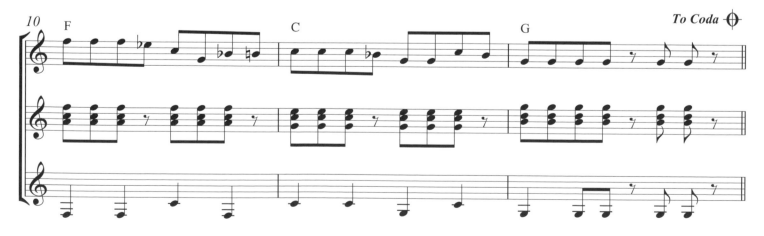

B

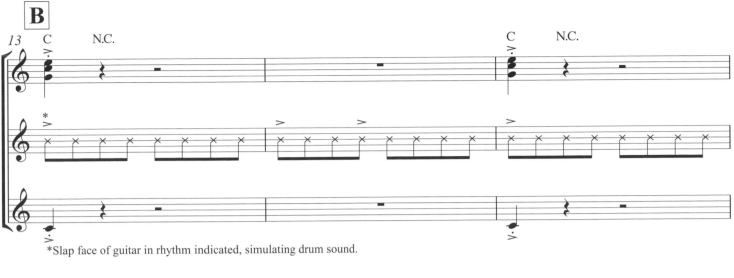

*Slap face of guitar in rhythm indicated, simulating drum sound.

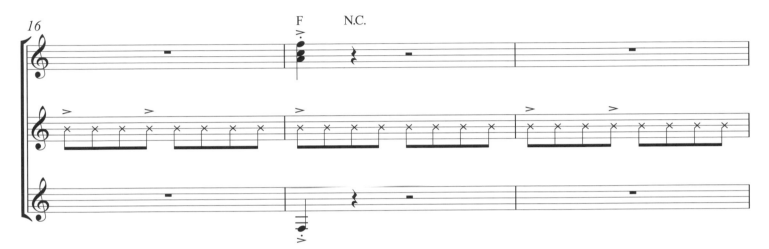

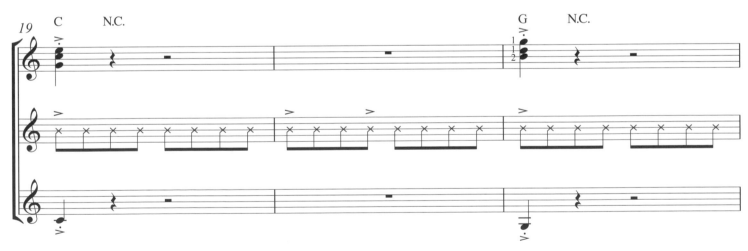

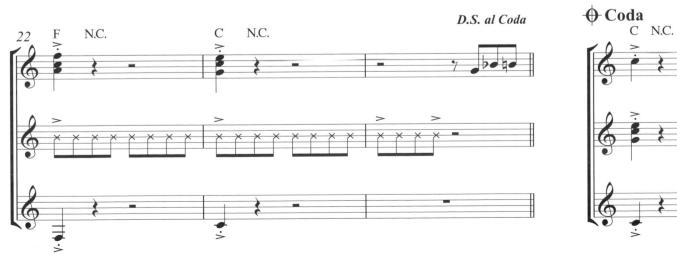

D.S. al Coda

Coda

ESSENTIAL ELEMENTS FOR GUITAR, BOOK 1

Comprehensive Guitar Method
by Will Schmid and Bob Morris

Take your guitar teaching to a new level! With the time-tested classroom teaching methods of Will Schmid and Bob Morris, popular songs in a variety of styles, and quality demonstration and backing tracks on the accompanying CD, *Essential Elements for Guitar* is a staple of guitar teachers' instruction – and helps beginning guitar students off to a great start.

This method has been designed to meet the National Standards for Music Education, with features such as cross-curricular activities, quizzes, multicultural songs, basic improvisation and more. Concepts covered in Book 1 include: getting started; basic music theory; guitar chords; notes on each string; music history; ensemble playing; performance spotlights; and much more!

Songs used in Book 1 include such hits as: Dust in the Wind • Eleanor Rigby • Every Breath You Take • Hey Jude • Hound Dog • Let It Be • Ode to Joy • Rock Around the Clock • Stand by Me • Surfin' USA • Sweet Home Chicago • This Land Is Your Land • You Really Got Me • and more!

00862639 Book/CD Pack $17.99

ESSENTIAL ELEMENTS FOR GUITAR, BOOK 2

Bob Morris

Essential Elements for Guitar, Book 2 is a continuation of the concepts and skills taught in Book 1 and includes all of its popular features as well – great songs in a variety of styles, a high-quality audio CD with demonstration and backing tracks, quizzes, music history, music theory, and much more. Concepts taught in Book 2 include: Playing melodically in positions up the neck; Playing movable chord shapes up the neck; Playing scales and extended chords in different keys; More right-hand studies – fingerpicking and pick style; Improvisation in positions up the neck; Studying different styles through great song selections; and more!

00865010 Book/CD Pack $17.99

Essential Elements Guitar Ensembles

The songs in the Essential Elements Guitar Ensemble series are playable by three or more guitars. Each arrangement features the melody, a harmony part, and bass line in standard notation along with chord symbols. For groups with more than three or four guitars, the parts can be doubled. This series is perfect for classroom guitar ensembles or other group guitar settings.

THE BEATLES
00865008 Early Intermediate Level......................$9.99

BOSSA NOVA
00865006 Intermediate/Advanced Level.......................$9.99

CHRISTMAS CLASSICS
00865015 Mid-Intermediate Level $9.99

CHRISTMAS SONGS
00001136 Mid-Beginner Level $9.95

CLASSICAL THEMES
00865005 Late Beginner Level......................$9.99

DISNEY SONGS
00865014 Early Intermediate Level......................$9.99

EASY POP SONGS
00865011 Mid-Beginner Level $9.99

DUKE ELLINGTON
00865009 Mid-Intermediate Level $9.99

GREAT THEMES
00865012 Mid-Intermediate Level $9.99

JIMI HENDRIX
00865013 Mid-Intermediate Level $9.99

JAZZ BALLADS
00865002 Early Intermediate Level......................$9.99

JAZZ STANDARDS
00865007 Mid-Intermediate Level $9.99

POP HITS
00001128 Late Beginner Level......................$9.99

ROCK CLASSICS
00865001 Late Beginner Level......................$9.95

Flash Cards

96 CARDS FOR BEGINNING GUITAR
00865000..$7.95

Essential Elements Guitar Repertoire Series

Hal Leonard's Essential Elements Guitar Repertoire Series features great original guitar music based on a style or theme that is carefully graded and leveled for easy selection. The songs are presented in standard notation and tablature, and are fully demonstrated on the accompanying CD.

TURBO ROCK
Beginner Intermediate Level
by Mark Huls
00001076 Book/CD Pack $9.95

BLUES CRUISE
Mid-Intermediate Level
by Dave Rubin
00000470 Book/CD Pack $9.95

MYSTERIOSO
Mid-Intermediate Level
by Allan Jaffe
00000471 Book/CD Pack $9.95

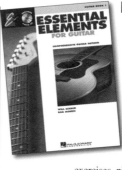

DAILY GUITAR WARM-UPS

by Tom Kolb
Mid-Beginner to Late Intermediate
This book contains a wide variety of exercises to help get your hands in top playing shape. It addresses the basic elements of guitar warm-ups by category: stretches and pre-playing coordination exercises, picking exercises, right and left-hand synchronization, and rhythm guitar warm-ups.
00865004 Book/CD Pack $9.99

Essential Elements Guitar Songs

The books in the Essential Elements Guitar Songs series feature popular songs specially selected for the practice of specific guitar chord types. Each book includes eight great songs and a CD with fantastic sounding play-along tracks. Practice at any tempo with the included Amazing Slow Downer software!

POWER CHORD ROCK
Mid-Beginner Level
00001139 Book/CD Pack $12.99

OPEN CHORD ROCK
Mid-Beginner Level
00001138 Book/CD Pack $12.99

BARRE CHORD ROCK
Late Beginner Level
00001137 Book/CD Pack $12.99

FOR MORE INFORMATION, SEE YOUR LOCAL MUSIC DEALER, OR WRITE TO:

HAL•LEONARD®
CORPORATION
7777 W. BLUEMOUND RD. P.O. BOX 13819 MILWAUKEE, WI 53213

Prices, contents, and availability subject to change without notice.

0513